V

ADVICE ON

HIP DYSPLASIA

IN DOGS

Gary Clayton Jones
BVetMed, DVR, DSAO, MRCVS.

ABOUT THE AUTHOR

Gary Clayton Jones qualified from the Royal Veterinary College London in 1965. He became a lecturer in the department of surgery at the College Field Station, finally becoming senior lecturer, and was appointed the first director of the Queen Mother Hospital for Animals. After 25 years teaching and operating at the university, Gary left to work in private practice. He now provides referrals and operates on numerous orthopaedic cases, including hip replacements, and runs a radiographic reporting service. He also consults in a number of practices in London.

Gary obtained a Diploma in Veterinary Radiology from the Royal College of Veterinary Surgeons (RCVS) and later was a Foundation Diplomat in Small Animal Orthopaedics. He has been active in the British Veterinary Association and has been Chief Scrutineer of the Hip Dysplasia scheme. He was the first UK chairman of the veterinary section of the AO/ASIF International Association for the Study of Internal Fixation.

ACKNOWLEDGEMENTS

Many thanks to Hill's Pet Nutrition for the use of their *Atlas of Veterinary Clinical Anatomy* for the line-drawings on pages 7, 15, 16, 20. Other line-drawings by Viv Rainsbury (pages 35, 36). X-rays courtesy of the author (pages 17, 40, 45).

Published by Ringpress Books,
a division of Interpet Publishing,
Vincent Lane, Dorking, Surrey, RH4 3YX, UK.
Tel: 01306 873822   Fax: 01306 876712
email: sales@interpet.co.uk

First published 2004
© 2004 Ringpress Books. All rights reserved.

ISBN 1 86054 227 1

Printed and bound in Singapore by Kyodo Printing

10 9 8 7 6 5 4 3 2 1

CONTENTS

Introduction

Sadly, there can't be a dog owner in the world who hasn't heard of hip dysplasia – the abnormal development of the hip joint.

In many ways, the condition can be considered the scourge of modern dog breeding. Wolves and wild dogs relied on good mobility for survival. A lame or slow dog was soon a hungry dog – and then a dead one.

Then, when man started to domesticate the species, dogs were bred for function – to herd sheep, retrieve game, or hunt prey – only the fittest animals were kept and bred from. Those not up to the job were culled.

Today, the dog's 'job' is mainly as a companion, and so the strict selection procedures of old are no longer in place. Now, we tend to select for temperament and looks, rather than for performance. Generally, this is a good thing, but it has meant that we are now seeing diseases and conditions that weren't previously problematic.

Hip dysplasia can affect all dogs – of whatever age, breed or size, although it mainly affects larger, pedigree dogs. The 12 worst-affected breeds are as follows:

In the UK, under the KC/BVA scheme:
1. Otterhound
2. Clumber Spaniel
3. Sussex Spaniel
4. Bullmastiff
5. Newfoundland
6. Gordon Setter
7. St. Bernard

8. Briard
9. Old English Sheepdog
10. English Setter
11. Golden Retriever
12. Welsh Springer Spaniel

In the US, under the Orthopedic Foundation for Animals scheme:
1. Bulldog
2. Pug
3. Dogue de Bordeaux
4. Otterhound
5. Clumber Spaniel
6. St. Bernard
7. Neapolitan Mastiff
8. Sussex Spaniel
9. Boykin Spaniel
10. Cane Corso Mastiff
11. American Bulldog
12. French Bulldog

For the complete lists, which are regularly updated, visit www.bva.co.uk and www.ofa.org

Human intervention may have exacerbated the disease, but we are now working to mend our errors. Through X-ray examination and scoring schemes, breeders are beginning to control hip dysplasia. Veterinary advances too, mean that a diagnosis of hip dysplasia is not as devastating as it once was.

This book, written by a leading specialist, tells you everything you need to know about this crippling disease, its causes and treatments. But of course, no publication can be a substitute for consultation with your own vet.

1 Anatomy of the hip joint

The hip joint is a diarthrodial joint of the ball-and-socket type. It consists of two components: the cup or acetabulum, which is part of the pelvis, and the femur head or caput, a ball that lies on the upper end of the femur shaft.

The surface of the acetabulum is lined with articular cartilage except for a small region in the lower portion, which has no cartilage. This area is the acetabular fossa. At the acetabular fossa, a ligament joins the femur head to the cup. This ligament is called the teres ligament. The fossa also contains a small amount of fat, which aids joint lubrication.

The femur head is part of the top of the thigh bone – the femur – and is attached to a portion of bone that arises from the shaft, called the femur neck.

The femur neck does not arise from the shaft of the femur at right angles, but is angled upwards and turned forwards. These angles are termed the angles of inclination and anteversion. They are important as they help to provide the best range of motion in the hip.

The femur head is quite rounded and is also covered by articular cartilage, except for a small cavity opposite the fossa called the fovea capitis, into which the other end of the teres ligament is attached.

MOVEMENT RANGE

Unlike a hinge-type joint (such as the elbow), a ball-and-socket joint enables a wide range of motion in many planes. A normal dog can run, jump, turn sharply, sit and stand. Without a ball-and-socket joint,

BALL-AND-SOCKET HIP JOINT

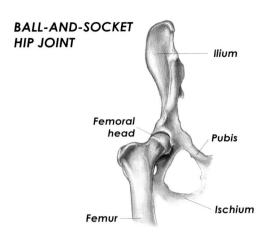

Ilium

Femoral head

Pubis

Ischium

Femur

the range of movement would be limited.

The hip can be moved forward into flexion, or extended backwards into extension; it may be drawn in towards the body in adduction or moved away from the body in abduction, as well as rotated. It allows motion in a forwards or backward direction while allowing the body to be turned at the same time.

The femur head is set at an angle, a little away from the shaft on the femur neck. This further increases the range of motion in the joint. So, the forces that are transferred up the leg as the stifle (knee) and the hock joints are straightened, lift the pelvis and the hind portion of the body, and allow forward propulsion of the body at a rapid rate.

MOTION CONTROLS

The motion of the hip joint is controlled by a number of mechanisms – in particular, to slow and brake the joint in a controlled manner as the joint surfaces reach the limits of motion. If this did not occur, then there would be a sudden, large force exerted when the joint stopped moving, which could result in damage to the joint structures.

The shapes of the acetabular surface and the femur head are not perfectly circular but are compound curves. The joint naturally brakes when it reaches the intended limits of motion, as the surfaces become progressively and gradually more locked together.

The motion of the head in the acetabulum is also controlled by the teres ligament, whose individual fibres tend to tighten as they twist together, and also by the fibres in the joint capsule becoming more tense.

MOVEMENT AND STABILITY

The joint has to be mobile but it must also be kept stable to prevent abnormal stresses from causing damage. This is achieved by the surfaces in a normal joint all fitting together accurately. However, for motion to be possible, the joint needs a small amount of laxity. So, a very narrow space – the joint cavity – remains between the surfaces. This is filled by a lubricating fluid – the joint or synovial fluid.

SYNOVIAL FLUID

This sticky, thick, clear substance is made by the synovial membrane and forms a complete, but very thin, film over the cartilage surfaces of a normal joint. Apart from providing lubrication, it also tends to hold the surfaces together by capillary force.

The joint surfaces are enclosed by a joint capsule, which has a number of important functions. It secretes the joint fluid from its inner layer of cells – the synoviocytes. This fluid lubricates the joint and also nourishes the cartilage cells on the surfaces of the joint.

Cartilage itself contains no blood vessels. Therefore, the cells rely entirely on the constantly replenished joint fluid (which obtains its nutrients from the blood circulating in the joint capsule vessels) to bring in all the essential nutrients and oxygen for their metabolism, and also to remove potentially harmful waste products that are formed. Cells within the joint fluid also help to reconstruct damaged areas and to remove fragments that may result from wear and tear or injury.

The combination of cartilage cells and the fibres in which they lie forms a complex surface. It feels very smooth and slippery to the touch, but it actually contains many fine crevices parallel to the surface of the joint. These crevices trap the joint fluid, enabling a very thin film to cover all the cartilage surface.

The fluid is a complex mixture of substances, including long chains of protein. These chains mesh together when the joint is at rest to form a fluid layer that is so sticky that it prevents the cartilage surfaces from becoming pressed together. When the joint begins to move, the meshed clumps of protein stretch out into long chains that can slide against each other. They maintain a complete layer over the cartilage, enabling the joint surfaces to move smoothly and rapidly.

Synovial fluid is a unique lubricant that works to protect the joint surfaces whether the joint is still, or whether it is undergoing slow or fast motion with equal efficiency. Its correct production is therefore essential to the maintenance of a healthy joint.

JOINT CAPSULE

The outer layer of the joint capsule is a supporting structure of fibrous-type tissue cells. It keeps the joint fluid in the joint cavity, assists in holding the joint components together, and supports the secreting layers within. It supports the blood vessels that enter and leave, and also contains nerve fibres that are both sensitive to pain and that warn the animal if the joint is being subjected to excessive stress.

MUSCLE SUPPORT

Outside the joint are the muscles and their tendons that move the joint. These muscles arise from the bones of the pelvis and spine around the acetabulum and are attached around the femur head on the upper outer portion of the femur that acts as a lever, called the trochanter. The main group moving the hip are the well-developed gluteus muscles.

Not only do muscles move the joint, but they also provide stability by retaining the head within the joint cavity by their tension. Muscles must be large and well trained to work in the most efficient manner. They are influenced by nutrition and exercise, and require a good nerve and blood supply to function properly.

Factors that affect the hip's function include:
• Size, shape and depth of the acetabulum
• Size and shape of the femur head
• Accuracy of the fit at the joint surfaces
• Laxity between the femur head and the acetabulum
• Length and angles of inclination of the femur neck
• Strength of the joint capsule
• Size and function of the muscles and tendons.

GROWTH OF THE HIP JOINT

It is important that the joints grow properly, to ensure they become large enough to support the adult animal. Dogs grow very quickly. Small puppies may weigh just a few hundred grams at birth, but can reach 50kg or more by 12 months of age when the skeleton has all but ceased growing.

During that time, the joint must grow adequately at all times to allow sufficient distribution of weight over the cartilage surface, so that no one point will become overloaded and damaged. The underlying bone must also be sufficiently large and strong to bear the weight of the body through the joint surfaces. However, it must also allow the animal to be active, and watching a puppy at play will reveal the enormous stresses that are placed on the growing skeleton of a young, boisterous animal.

The acetabulum forms at the junction of three bones on each side, which all join to create the single bone known as the pelvis. In a puppy, these bones link at the middle of the acetabular surface with a thin interface of cartilage. Cartilage cells multiply more rapidly than bone, so they enable the acetabular cavity to enlarge as much as is needed as the puppy grows.

The head of the femur is initially separated from the femur neck by a layer of cartilage – the growth plate. Growth plate cells multiply and allow the femur neck to elongate. The head the juvenile femur, the caput, is composed of bone covered by cartilage cells, which can grow in diameter as the cartilage cells multiply.

As the cells multiply, the deeper layers of cartilage become replaced and transformed into bone. This is necessary, as cartilage is not as strong as bone and it could be deformed by pressure if it was too thick.

The shapes of the acetabulum and the femur head are intimately related. The pressure of the femur head, as well as its motion in the acetabulum, determines the shape and curves of the acetabulum. Similarly, the shape and curvature of the femur head depend on it being contained in – and moving within – the cup.

If something goes wrong during the growth period, even for a short time, the shapes of the joint components may be irretrievably altered. Of course, this will then affect how the joint may function. If the joint surfaces and shapes are not correctly formed, then they will also be liable to abnormal stresses and strains, which may lead to joint disease, such as arthritis.

2 Hip dysplasia: the disease

Dysplasia comes from the two Greek words 'dys', meaning 'abnormal', and 'plassein', meaning 'growth'.

Hip dysplasia is thought to start in animals that may begin with a normal joint at birth. The initial change is an excessive degree of joint laxity. It is not known why this occurs, but it could be caused by the acetabulum or the femur head failing to develop and/or some deficiency in the supporting joint tissues. It is generally agreed to be an inherited disease problem.

Suggested causes include:

- Shallow acetabulum
- Abnormal femur head or neck angulation
- Insufficient muscle mass
- Neuromuscular disease of some of the adductor muscles of the hip
- Lack of vitamin C or ascorbic acid
- Abnormal sex hormone levels
- Excessive exercise or activity
- Obesity or over rapid growth during a critical period
- Injury
- Abnormal relationship to other bones and hind leg joints
- Genetic influence.

Whatever the cause, the looseness of the joint then begins to place excessive strain on the joint capsule, damaging its microstructures and causing inflammation.

The swelling of the capsule also results in a reduced ability of motion in the joint, and joint stiffness. The nerve cells within the capsule also become stimulated, causing hip pain.

ABNORMAL JOINT FLUID
Part of this process of inflammation is the formation of abnormal joint fluid. The fluid is no longer such a good lubricant, because it becomes more watery, contains inflammatory products, such as proteins and inflammatory cells, and does not contain the correct nutrients.

The fluid no longer provides such good capillary attraction between the joint surfaces because its physical properties are altered, so the joint surfaces are now looser against each other. This means the femur head is no longer pressed into the acetabulum, and the acetabulum no longer captures the femur head. As these bones grow larger, the acetabulum becomes shallower and the femur head becomes less round as the normal moulding pressures from one bone pressing into the other are reduced.

As the joint moves, the load on the articular cartilage is no longer evenly distributed, so that certain areas become subjected to excessive stress. As the cartilage already has a faulty lubrication system, its surface begins to wear away. The worn fragments of cartilage are then released into the joint fluid and these act as a focus for the development of further inflammation.

The increased volume of the inflamed joint fluid may also help to contribute to instability in the joint, as it tends to force the joint surfaces apart. Thus, once the problem begins, it becomes a vicious cycle with each abnormality helping to create further changes.

SUBTLE SIGNS
During this time, there can be one paradox – when watched, the puppy may not show any obvious signs.

The effects of a slightly lax joint may be imperceptible, so the puppy appears normal. However, as the joint becomes more lax, signs may become more noticeable. For example, as the dog tries to rise, the forces on the joint as the limb extends do not initially raise the hip (and thus the hind end of the body) upwards, but the femur head is just displaced out a little from the acetabulum. The dog will then only begin to rise once sufficient force is applied to make the joint structures become sufficiently tense and stable again, so the dog appears to be making an excessive effort to get up.

The joint capsule will not initially be painful, but once inflammation is established, it may become so, and the dog may show signs of discomfort when he tries to move. Cartilage with superficial worn areas is not painful, as it does not contain any nerve endings; only when the deeper structure is penetrated will the underlying pain receptors be affected.

CHANGING GAIT

Once the initial phase of laxity becomes established, the dog has to try to compensate for the lack of hip control and the abnormal motion by altering his gait.

Often, a rolling gait is developed. This is the result of the joints being unstable in a side-to-side motion as the dog walks or because the dog tries to walk without moving the hips as he would normally, because they are painful. The lower portion of the back is flexed from side to side, which enables him to advance even though the hips move through a smaller range of motion. The reduced hip movement results in the stifle and hock joints also tending to move less, so that the hind legs are maintained in a rather straightened position.

This laxity in the hips can often be felt as a clicking

NORMAL HIP JOINT

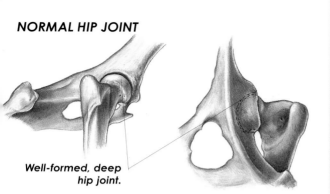

Well-formed, deep hip joint.

sensation as the dog walks along, by resting the fingers on the hips while walking behind the dog as he is encouraged to move forwards. Arching of the back also transfers more of the weight on to the forelegs, which reduces the strain and therefore any pain in the hip joints. Over a period of time, the forelegs may become more developed than normal because of the extra work they have to perform. Correspondingly, as the hind legs do less work, they become underdeveloped, so the front and back of the dog become more poorly matched.

REMODELLING PROCESS

The body's natural response is to try to limit joint laxity as the dog grows, and a number of mechanisms come into play. Initially, the edges of the acetabulum are overloaded and become worn and deformed. As the deeper parts of the acetabulum are no longer filled by the femur head, bone growth can occur and the deeper portions of the cavity begin to be infilled.

The edges of the acetabulum, which are now being very stressed, respond by trying to repair the damage. Extra bone is formed at the margins, in order to increase the bone strength. This results in a more saucer-shaped acetabulum developing.

Shallow hip joint with subluxated femoral head in younger dogs.

The femur head, which is no longer enclosed within the cavity, grows and becomes more flattened in shape until, ultimately, the femur head and acetabular surfaces will tend to match one another once more.

The excessive stresses placed on the joint capsule result in inflammation; part of the inflammatory process is that the supporting structures of the capsule become more thickened by the formation of more connective tissue. Thus the capsule can begin to take more of the strain and contribute once more to stabilisation.

A thick joint capsule obviously needs a greater area of bone to which it can be attached, so new bone also begins to form around the margins of the joint at the capsular attachment.

Damaged articular cartilage may also undergo attempts at repair. Young cartilage cells are able to multiply, so that, provided the forces of wear and tear are not too excessive, the cartilage cells may restore at least some of the surface.

Where the cartilage is very worn, then the underlying bone becomes exposed and will harden (become sclerotic). This can result in the contained pain sensors becoming compressed and non-functional, so that pain is not so evident. However, eroded

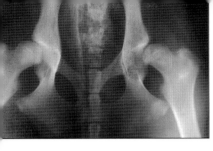

Remodelling process: this six-month-old Golden Retriever's hips are partially displaced but just remain within the margin of the acetabulum, which is widened and remodelled. As yet, little new growth has formed on the joint margins.

cartilage can present a chronic problem because the exposed underlying bone surfaces have much higher levels of friction than cartilage (the bony surface is not so well lubricated). Therefore, joint motion is impeded.

During this remodelling process, the teres ligament will also be affected. It can become swollen and weakened as it takes the excessive strain, and, in a small number of cases, it can actually rupture. If this should occur, it is often noticed at around eight months of age. This will result in the femur head becoming more lax and unstable once again, so that lameness will worsen until further remodelling has stabilised the joint once more.

Remodelling is a continuous process, which hits its peak by the time the dog reaches skeletal maturity at around 15 months of age, although some remodelling will continue throughout life. The rate of remodelling may become very slow after skeletal maturity. The amount of lameness displayed during this time will depend on a number of factors, such as the rate at which the dog gains weight, the amount of joint cartilage erosion and muscle development, the type and vigour of exercise, and whether any medication is being given, and of what type.

The signs of hip dysplasia depend on how much discomfort and laxity is present, and therefore how much lameness the dog may show. Sometimes, surprisingly advanced degrees of dysplasia may be found when the dog is radiographed, but the signs of lameness can be minimal. The dog is able to adapt remarkably well to a problem, especially if it is symmetrical in both legs and may be concealed to even the most expert eye. X-rays, therefore, are essential.

Initially, clinical signs will result from instability in the hip joint, and then may progress as a result of inflammation of the affected joint structures – arthritis.

RELUCTANCE TO RISE

In clinical cases, the first sign is generally a reluctance to rise, and possibly mild and transient stiffness following a period of rest. The dog will try to lift himself by making more use of the forelegs and by arching his back. A somewhat wobbly hind leg action may be seen.

The dog may also vocalise that he is in pain when he attempts to move. Clearly, this will be more obvious in a heavy dog than in a lighter one. Thus the breed type, size of puppy, and amount of weight the dog has, as well as the rate of the weight gain, will all be variable factors that come into effect. A light-weight, slow-growing dog may have fewer signs than an overweight fast-growing puppy of the same breed.

Dogs that are exercising sufficiently to develop good hind limb muscles will have more stability and may therefore have fewer signs than a less fit animal. Later, the dog may show more signs of discomfort, and may even cry when trying to move or turn. It may be painful if knocked, and stiffness following rest may last a longer time or even be constant.

MOVEMENT AND GAIT

As the dog does less, his muscle mass over the hips appears underdeveloped while the muscles of the forelegs appear overdeveloped.

The hind legs often have more of an upright stance because the stifle and hock joints are not flexed as they would be if the dog was weight-bearing fully. The hind legs are held by the dog so that the feet tend to become rather close together – adducted – and the hind leg stride length shortened.

When moving, the hind legs often bunny-hop once the dog tries to move more rapidly than the walking pace, and the dog will sway from side to side.

When turning, the dog may fall over on the hind legs. The hips appear prominent, and clicking may be heard or felt as the dog moves. In a small number of cases, one or both hip joints may actually become dislocated, often following only a minor accident.

CORRECT DIAGNOSIS

Many of the signs described are similar or identical to those seen in other diseases, and veterinary investigation and tests, such as X-rays or muscle or nerve examination, will be required.

Clinical problems that may be confused with HD in young dogs:
- Osteochondrosis dissecans (OCD) of the stifle joint
- Patellar luxation (dislocation of the knee-cap)
- OCD of the hock joints
- Panosteitis (puppy lameness due to inflammation/

necrosis of the bone marrow)
- Various developmental disorders of the neuromuscular system
- Numerous spinal abnormalities, including cervical spondylopathy (Wobbler disease of young dogs).

THE OLDER DOG

In the older dog, the signs are primarily the result of developing degenerative joint disease (DJD) rather than instability. There is a tendency for the dysplastic joint to become stable by maturity. However, this does not prevent wear and tear occurring more rapidly than in a normal dog, and these effects will be seen as arthritis of the hip joint.

A common difficulty in the mature dog is that clinical signs related to the hind legs can develop as a result of many other disorders that may exist at the same time as HD.

It is important to recognise that a large number of animals may have signs of HD on their radiographs but relatively few will show significant signs. Nevertheless, some animals do have clinical features that can be recognised.

Hip arthritis usually has a relatively slow progression.

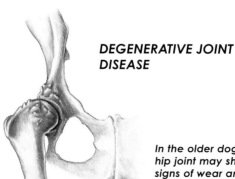

DEGENERATIVE JOINT DISEASE

In the older dog, the hip joint may show signs of wear and tear.

We expect older dogs to 'slow up' as a result of the general ageing process, so we may accept some general loss of function as being natural. Difficulty in rising, stiffness after rest, a less mobile hind limb action, and less exercise tolerance can all be seen.

Affected dogs may have more difficulty with stairs, when jumping on furniture or into the car, and may also show signs of pain by crying, whimpering, or just by being unable to settle when lying or sitting. Carrying the leg is not usually associated with hip arthritis from HD and usually results from some other hip condition or from disease in a different joint.

In a small number of cases, the hip joint may become dislocated following a minor injury. Clicking (crepitus) of the hip joints may also be heard or felt.

Conditions that may be confused with HD in the older dog:

Nervous system disorders
- Spinal problems such as: chronic dorsal radicular myelopathy (CDRM), or degenerative myelopathy
- Disc disease, including Wobbler syndrome
- Abnormalities of the vertebrae – resulting in a change of shape or arthritis of the spinal joints
- Lumbrosacral diseases (those affecting the area between the dog's lower back and his sacral bone at the start of his tail)
- Spinal tumours and other disorders are rarer diseases that might occasionally be seen.

Orthopaedic problems include:
- Stifle joint (knee) disorders
- Disorders or the Achilles tendon mechanism near the hock joint
- Arthritis of the hock joint.

4 Non-surgical treatment

The successful treatment of hip dysplasia can be achieved in many cases by so-called conservative means. These are the first line of attack that should be employed in every case, before surgical options (see Chapter Five) are considered.

YOUNG ANIMALS
In these cases, the early signs will be partly mechanical and the result of joint laxity and partly from pain associated with this laxity and secondary erosion or inflammation of the joint. The first thing to do is to control and reduce the overall stress on the joint.

DIET AND OBESITY
The weight of the dog is something that can readily be evaluated and corrected. If the dog is overweight, then the amount of food being given may be reduced, ensuring that a balanced diet is maintained (suitable complete diets are now readily available – ask your vet for details). It is best to monitor your dog's weight by weighing him weekly (using the same scales each time) and recording the result on a chart.

Your vet will tell you your dog's ideal weight. However, as there is considerable variation in individual size even within a breed, then assessment of the individual is very important. Excess fat is present if:
• The waistline is not visible
• The dog has a pot-bellied appearance
• The ribs are not easily apparent when feeling over the ribcage.

Obesity subjects the joint to stress so it is essential that a dog is kept fit and lean (as above).

For dogs with severe signs, then significant weight loss may be of great value, as this will reduce the load on the abnormal joints. Some dogs appear to grow very quickly and this places considerable strain on the skeleton. The rate of weight gain will depend on the food quality and quantity that the dog consumes as well as how active he is. Of course, as the joints become painful so the dog becomes less active, less energy is used and therefore the dog will conserve the unused energy as fat. So, what was adequate food for an active dog can be too much for an inactive dog of the same size.

Some commercial foods are designed to encourage a rapid weight gain. This is satisfactory, provided the dog is normal, but such foods may need to be used with caution if there is a problem. Balancing the diet may be achieved by changing from a puppy to juvenile food, or from juvenile to adult slightly earlier than recommended if there is a growth problem. Altering home-made diets is much more complicated than feeding commercial diets.

Ideas such as not giving the dog any biscuit meal and only giving meat products are not correct. It is important that a balance between carbohydrate, protein and vitamins and minerals etc., is maintained, regardless of the quantity of food being given. Similarly, the use of treats in training should not be stopped in an attempt to reduce weight gain. Treats are acceptable, provided they are rationed and the owner remembers to include them as part of the overall diet.

It is difficult to give hard-and-fast rules as to how quickly an individual dog should grow, and previous experience of raising a puppy and asking other people (breeder and vets) may be useful. There are some published charts that can be used as a general guide – they are available either through your vet or from the dog food companies. The problem is that the damage to the joints may already be done by a very early rapid growth rate, and slowing the rate down later is rather like closing the door after the horse has bolted. However, it is still one thing that will contribute to helping the problem.

CONTROLLED EXERCISE

Activity can be controlled in terms of duration, frequency and type. The object of activity is to encourage the development of suitable muscle strength to provide some support to the joint. Activity is also important for the overall development of the dog, in terms of his relationships with people and other dogs, as well as reducing the chances of behavioural problems from occurring as a result of boredom or failure of training.

Resting and confining the dog does not encourage muscle development; movement of all the joints during growth is essential to encourage muscle growth with as good a range of motion as possible. Attempts to confine activity 24 hours a day will simply result in the dog attempting 'the wall of death' round the room, when he may do more damage than if he had been allowed some controlled activity.

The best exercise is slow walking on the lead. This forces the dog to use each leg individually – if left free, he would tend to bunny hop, which is not beneficial for the hind leg musculature.

For severely lame individuals, a suitable regime to begin with may be about four five-minute walks spread throughout the day. As the dog improves, then the duration of each walk may be increased by about five minutes per walk per week, as a rough rule of thumb. In general, if the length of the walk makes the

Slow walking on the lead encourages the use of all hind limb muscles.

dog more lame, then it should be shortened. In many respects, the frequency of walks is more important than the duration, as resting will often be followed by a period of stiffness when rising – 'stiffness after rest'. This is reduced and shortened by regular but short periods of activity through the day.

CONSERVATIVE SUCCESS

The overall result of conservative management in young dogs is approximately 75 per cent – i.e. three in four puppies with clinical signs of hip dysplasia will improve to become satisfactory by the time they reach skeletal maturity at about 15 months of age.

Many of these animals will then go on to have a reasonable quality of life with little sign of discomfort and the ability to manage moderate exercise, although perhaps not full athleticism. They will have a risk of developing signs of degenerative joint disease (DJD) in later life, but, in practice, the proportion of these dogs requiring major interventions seems to be small – perhaps as low as 10 per cent of animals.

Thus the conservative treatment of young dogs can achieve a high standard of success in many cases while surgery (see Chapter Five) remains a possible option for the small number who fail to improve or who require treatment in later life.

OLDER ANIMALS

A conservative approach is often valuable for older animals, and can also be successful in a significant proportion of patients. The cornerstones of treatment are aimed at managing the secondary effects of the disease – degenerative joint disease (DJD) or arthritis. These cornerstones are: bodyweight, exercise and medication.

BODYWEIGHT

A dog's bodyweight commonly rises as he gets older. Reasons for this include: hormonal effects following neutering; and/or underlying medical problems (e.g. hypothyroidism), heart or respiratory disease, as well as disorders that lead to a gradually reduced exercise tolerance. Failure to adapt the dog's diet to his reduced activity level will lead to significant weight gain.

A reduction of bodyweight can be achieved by dietary control. This can be done by switching to a commercial low-calorie diet. In addition, many vets offer a weight control service, usually managed by vet nurses specially trained in nutritional management. Pets in their care will be regularly weighed and monitored, which is essential to successful dietary control.

In the home, similar results can be achieved by weighing the dog regularly every one to two weeks and maintaining a weight chart. To feed the dog, the normal food – including all extra tidbits – must be weighed, and then the total quantity being offered must be reduced by about one fifth to one quarter. The reduction should involve all items of food in equal proportion to maintain the balance in the diet.

Stopping all treats is not ideal, as the dog then imagines he is being punished. The tidbits should be carefully rationed and considered part of the diet. Thus they also need reducing in quantity. This regime will achieve a gradual weight loss in most animals. For those cases that are severely overweight or have had a major reduction in their exercise pattern, a further food reduction may be required if no weight loss is noted within a month of starting the diet.

It is surprising how little food an overweight dog needs to consume each day to maintain a constant bodyweight.

Careful exercise management is required for the arthritic older dog.

EXERCISE

The dog's exercise will also need to be adapted to avoid prolonged periods of activity followed by long periods of rest. Short but frequent periods of activity are much better for joint function.

Exercise the dog on a flatter area, not on stony beaches or in thick mud or over fallen trees. The level of activity should remain constant each day and not be shorter during the week or longer at the weekend. Non-weightbearing activity, such as hydrotherapy, may also be useful, especially if the dog enjoys water.

PRESCRIPTION MEDICATION

Medication is also available for the older patient, but may be needed for long or even continual periods in some animals, if surgery is not an option. In general, non-steroidal drugs are preferred to those that contain cortico steroids, and dosing regimes may need to be altered to suit the individual patient.

In general, the manufacturer's recommended dose rate should be taken as a guide and should certainly not be exceeded; however, often a lower dose may be effective. Sometimes half or less of the original dose will be adequate and the dose can always be raised if needed. Medication can be tried on a less frequent schedule than recommended, say every alternate day.

The time of day at which medication is given can also be varied to suit the individual. Stiffness after rest, and night-time restlessness may better be controlled by a dose later in the day, while difficulty exercising may be better managed by dosing earlier in the day, say about 20 minutes before taking the dog out for a walk.

Maintaining some form of pain or symptom chart associated with medication is also helpful for your vet to try to find the best drug programme for your dog.

Many owners become conditioned to giving the dog medication on a regular, continuous basis. Occasionally reducing or even stopping the medication can be useful to show that, in some cases, the medication is either ineffectual, is no longer required, or can be continued at a lower dose rate. For example, sometimes the dog experiences a short-term flare-up or inflammation – possibly after an excess period of activity or some form of injury – which then settles after a period of treatment, and the dog then reverts to his normal situation.

A variety of medications and methods have been used to alleviate the symptoms of HD. These include:
• Drugs and techniques to diminish the signs of inflammation
• Drugs and nutritional additives to maintain and improve joint cartilage
• Drugs and other agents that might influence growth.

Anti-inflammatory drugs
The most common form of medication for HD. They reduce inflammation and thereby reduce pain. Pain

usually arises from inflammation in the joint capsule and as a result of erosion in the joint cartilage exposing nerve endings beneath the surface. Chronic inflammation will result in an increase in blood supply to the underlying bone, and this causes increased pressure within the veins inside the bone, which can also be a cause of bone and joint pain.

a) Non-steroidal drugs (NSAIDS)

These are drugs that interfere with the chemical chain reactions that constitute inflammation. The differences between different drugs concern the exact level at which the inflammatory process is inhibited.

b) Cortico steroids

These are derived from cortisone, which is a natural compound found in the body. Various synthetic compounds are more effective than cortisone. Steroids have a very good effect in terms of reducing inflammation but have significant problems in terms of the side effects that they can produce and because they tend to impede any natural repair processes that might occur within the joint. With this, there is a tendency for cartilage erosions gradually to worsen under the effects of steroids.

Side effects develop because the presence of steroids in the body will inhibit the action of the adrenal glands in the body. Dogs will tend to eat and drink more, and may appear to have urinary incontinence. They may also develop hair loss over the trunk, increase in weight, develop a pot belly, become mentally and physically slower, and develop muscle weakness. These effects are to some extent related to the dose level and frequency of dosing needed.

Steroids are generally advised mainly for immune-mediated types of arthritis, such as rheumatoid arthritis, which are not usually a type of inflammation associated with hip dysplasia.

c) Cartilage-sparing drugs
These reduce inflammation and enable damaged areas of cartilage to repair.

ANTI-INFLAMMATORY AGENTS:	
Non-steroidal	**Cortico steroids**
Aspirin	Betamethazone
Carprophen	Dexamethazone
Phenylbutazone	Prednisolone
Piroxicam	Predno leucotropin
Paracetemol	Methylprednisolone
Flunixine	
Ketoprofen	**Cartilage-sparing**
Meloxicam	**drugs**
Vedaprofen	Cartrophen
Tofenamic acid	
Topoxalin	

'ALTERNATIVE' APPROACH

Non-prescription drugs
Glucosamine, chondroitin, essential fatty acid supplements, and liver oils contain the components of articular cartilage in the form that could be assimilated by the damaged cartilage and thereby aid its repair. It is also possible that such compounds may enable cartilage to grow in a better manner.

Unfortunately, none of these claims have much scientific basis in fact and no controlled trials have been performed. It is probable that, at best, they would have a marginal benefit, although some cases do appear to make some improvement. These agents appear to have few side effects and little evidence that they may be harmful.

Acupuncture
Scientific tests have established that acupuncture may be of benefit in reducing pain, and it has been employed for this purpose in HD. The procedure is relatively benign; although it might not be very effective, it has not been shown to do any harm.

Hydrotherapy
This non-weightbearing exercise – enjoyed by many dogs – encourages muscle development without concussion in the joint that could damage the cartilage surfaces and the joint edges. It also encourages a good range of joint movement.

Homoeopathy
This is a form of medication using very minute doses of substances, which, if given in large amounts, would produce signs of arthritis. It remains a controversial method of treatment but some vets can practise this form of medicine after special training. It is a therapy that can be tried without fear of side effects.

Unproved methods
Copper bangles and magnetic collars rely on the piezo electric effect in which components of the body cells may be influenced by electrical or magnetic fields in such a way that their realignment may have some therapeutic benefit. The mode of supposed action is controversial. Controlled trials are few and mainly relate to treating fractures. The evidence for their efficacy is largely anecdotal.

5 Surgical treatment

A variety of surgical procedures have been advocated for treatment and continue to be developed.

Operations may basically be divided into two groups:

- Those for young, immature animals are intended to modify the manner in which the hip joint grows
- Those for older animals salvage the joint after signs of arthritis have become established.

It is important to reserve surgical treatment for dogs that are showing clinical signs rather than to operate on a patient just because signs of HD are found on an X-ray examination. Many of the operations are major and require specialised training and instrumentation, and carry risks of complications that might be worse than the signs of the original disease.

PECTINEUS MUSCLE SECTION

The pectineus is an adductor muscle that lies on the inner aspect of the thigh, very close to the underside of the hip joint. It appears very tense in cases of HD. Pressure on the muscle will sometimes be very painful to the dog.

Various modifications of the operation have been devised and consist of cutting the pectineus muscle, cutting and/or removing a portion of its tendon, or removing the whole of the muscle and tendon.

Original reports of the procedure suggested that animals showed an almost instant relief from discomfort, but further work has shown that the number of dogs that show such a dramatic improvement is actually quite small. Many animals do slowly improve over a few weeks or months, but it is uncertain if these animals would have improved anyway with the changes in management that would be instituted as well (as described under conservative therapy, see Chapter Four).

X-ray studies have shown that pectineus operations do not affect the appearance of the joint or the subsequent development of HD after surgery, and the procedure in the UK is now less commonly performed. However, it is a low-risk operation that is very unlikely to make the condition worse.

PUBIC SYMPHYSEODESIS

This is a new operation, which needs to be carried out while puppies are still fairly young, probably before about 20 weeks of age. It consists of causing the pubic symphysis in the mid-line of the pelvis to fuse prematurely so as to cause the ventral (abdominal) aspect of the pelvis to become narrowed. As the remainder of the pelvis grows, the acetabulae become slightly rotated outwards, thus creating a deeper cup and stabilising the growing hip.

This operation has not yet been tried enough to know how successful it might be.

TRIPLE PELVIC OSTEOTOMY

Rotation of the acetabulum can be achieved by this procedure in a more defined manner. After an X-ray examination to ensure that the bony signs of arthritis are minimal or absent, the joint is evaluated to determine certain angles at which the joint dislocates and can be replaced. The operation is performed by cutting the pelvis at each hip joint in three places – hence the name.

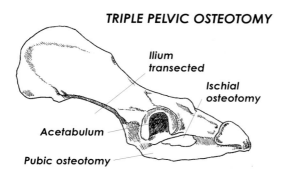

TRIPLE PELVIC OSTEOTOMY

Ilium transected

Ischial osteotomy

Acetabulum

Pubic osteotomy

The bony portion containing the acetabulum is released by cutting through the ilium in front of the socket, in the ischium behind it, and ventrally through the pubis. The released segment of bone is then rotated outwards to the angle assessed beforehand and then fixed into position using plates and screws. Special plates are available that have been designed specifically for this procedure.

Provided the operation is performed before significant arthritic reaction and remodelling have taken place and while the joint is unstable, then a fairly high success rate is achieved, although complications related to the implants are found in some cases. However, it is a very major procedure, particularly if both hips need to be operated on. As yet, it has not been proved that operated dogs will have a lower incidence of arthritis in later life.

FEMORAL NECK LENGTHENING

This is a procedure carried out by some surgeons usually in association with the triple osteotomy (above). The upper portion of the femur is split along the length to enable a wedge to be inserted and fixed into place with bone screws. This lengthens the neck of the femur, which will tend to push the femur head more firmly into the acetabulum and increase hip stability by increasing the tension in the thigh muscles. This correction also improves the biomechanical stresses on the hip and corrects the abnormally short femur neck that is found in some patients.

This procedure is not often performed as it is associated with considerable bleeding, and its overall success is not known.

INTERTROCHANTERIC VARISATION OSTEOTOMY

An osteotomy (bone-cutting operation) is performed just below the level of the femur neck region. A small triangular wedge of bone is then removed and the surfaces of the osteotomy are realigned so as to tilt the femur head further into the acetabulum.

The size of the wedge to be removed is calculated so as to bring the femur neck angle back to 135 degrees when the surfaces are repaired. Special instruments and a metal bone plate have been devised specifically for this procedure. The result is that there is an increased contact between the femur head surface and the acetabulum, similar to that obtained with the triple pelvic osteotomy (see page 34).

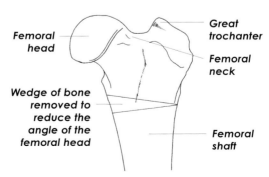

INTERTROCHANTERIC VARISATION OSTEOTOMY

It is also possible with this operation to correct any disturbance of the rotation of the femur neck (anteversion) which may have developed as a result of the dysplasia, by turning the femur head segment of bone backwards by the required angle before applying the plate and screws.

The success rate of this operation is somewhat lower than that recorded for triple pelvic osteotomy and it is a less popular operation than previously.

OSTEOTOMY OF THE ACETABULAR ROOF

This is another procedure devised to try to increase the amount of femur head that is contained by the acetabulum and thereby to reduce the joint laxity. A curved incision is made in the bone a few millimetres away from the edge of the acetabulum until the whole socket can be mobilised and rotated a little downwards. Bone graft is then harvested from the pelvis and packed into the bony incision to retain the acetabulum in the rotated position. This procedure has only been of limited popularity and has largely been replaced by the triple osteotomy (see page 34).

BOP PROCEDURE – SHELF ARTHROPLASTY

In this operation, a block of synthetic material is screwed to the acetabulum near to its upper, front edge. The material is termed Biocompatible Osteoconductive Polymer (BOP) and was developed as a substance that would allow bone growth and ultimately be absorbed by the body. It would therefore mean that obtaining a bone graft from another site was unnecessary. It is said to induce the formation of a bony reaction or shelf at the point where it is attached to the pelvis, which should then contribute to the stabilisation of the joint by extending the roof of the acetabulum.

The procedure has been controversial, with some people claiming significant success, while others have failed to demonstrate any significant benefits.

FEMORAL HEAD RESECTION (EXCISION ARTHROPLASTY)

Removal of the femur head is a long-established salvage procedure for a variety of diseases of the hip joint, and was used in humans before the advent of hip replacement. It is based on removing the femoral head and neck, and allowing the defect to heal so that the femur is only attached to the pelvis by flexible scar tissue. This removes one of the components that is rubbing and will usually significantly reduce pain.

In young dogs, recovery can be reasonably rapid, but it is usually much slower in older animals, when it may take a number of months. The end result may be some reduction in the range of hip joint motion and the operated leg will appear shorter than the unoperated leg in cases where HD affects only one side.

It is important, in all cases, to encourage the dog to use the leg as soon as possible after surgery, as the ultimate function and range of motion will depend on the flexibility of scar tissue that is formed. Enforced rest, other than for the immediate first day or two after the procedure, is counterproductive.

The best result is achieved using techniques that have minimal dissection of the tendons and muscles so that healing is rapid. Generally, the end result is somewhat dependent on the size of the dog – success rates tend to fall with the increasing size of the patient. In large breeds, there is a success rate of around 60 per cent. There is usually a better outcome in cases of severe lameness than in dogs with only a minor disability.

TOTAL HIP REPLACEMENT (THR)

This procedure is used far more than a few years ago because the recovery time from a replacement is much more rapid – now only about six weeks, with animals using the leg within days of surgery. There is usually no loss of leg length and an almost immediate reduction in pain. The physiotherapy needed following femoral head resection (page 38) is not usually required.

The development of artificial hip joint prostheses continues and there are now longlasting and effective implants commercially available to suit a variety of mainly medium-sized and larger animals. Small prostheses are also made, but generally, femoral head resection has a relatively high success rate in smaller animals (of 15 kg or less) so that THR is considered unnecessary in such patients and is technically more demanding than in larger animals.

The procedure for a total hip replacement involves removing the femur head, drilling a track in the femur shaft (reaming) so that a femoral component can be inserted; removing part of the acetabulum with a special reamer to cut away the cartilage and bone until a plastic or ceramic artificial cup (acetabular prosthesis) can be fitted. These are fixed in place with a special bone cement (perhaps impregnated with antibiotics), by screws, or by so-called cementless systems.

A total hip replacement is a demanding operation, requiring a high degree of technical skill and good facilities. In experienced hands, the success rate may well exceed 90 per cent.

Not all patients will be suitable for a hip replacement, and it is probably unwise to operate on immature animals. I prefer to operate after about 15 months of age, as the skeleton will have ceased growing and the bone will be well formed and able to accept the implants. There is a higher risk of complications in animals that have had previous hip surgery and those where there is a potential source of chronic infection, such as in dogs with skin disease.

Because the prosthetic hip is constructed from plastic and metal components, there is a risk that the artificial hip could wear itself out after some years, although a life expectancy of the joint of six to eight years is probably not unreasonable in most animals. Should the worn out artificial joint need replacing, then this can be a difficult operation and carry a significantly lower success rate, so, in many ways, patients of about four to six years may seem ideal.

However, old age is not a definite contraindication to surgery, as, provided the patient is otherwise well, the operation is similar in duration and success in young and old animals. The condition of the hip joint that is to be replaced is also relatively immaterial, as the bony parts are to be replaced by an artificial joint.

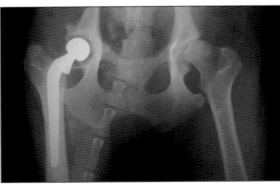

Post-operative X-ray of a hip replacement. The femur component is metal, so looks white on the X-ray. The acetabular component is plastic, so appears invisible – but it contains a small wire ring, so that its position can be seen. White bone cement is evident in the pelvic bone around the acetabulum.

6 Control methods

Methods to diminish the incidence of, or to eradicate, hip dysplasia have been attempted for more than 40 years. They are based on the view that the disease has an inherited (i.e. genetic) basis. So, affected parents will tend to transmit the condition to their offspring, and, in general, the greater the degree of dysplasia in the parents, the greater the degree of change found in the offspring.

Generally, it is also true that the better the parents, the better the offspring. Therefore, screening parental stock, to breed only unaffected animals, should diminish the incidence and severity of the condition.

The problem is that some animals have no physical signs of lameness and appear to be normal animals with a normal gait, but, if X-rayed, would be found to have marked changes. There is therefore no indication to the breeder that such animals may, in fact, be carrying the genes of hip dysplasia and might then pass on the problem, unless they go to the trouble of having the dog or bitch tested by X-ray examination.

SCREENING METHODS

A variety of methods have been used to try to screen the parental stock. Evaluating adult animals on the basis of function (e.g. how they perform in the show ring), or by manipulating the hip joints for laxity, are either unsuccessful or so inaccurate as to be of little value. As yet, no blood test for DNA analysis exists for this condition.

The most widely used forms of screening are based

on examining X-rays of the hip joints. This is generally carried out on adult dogs, as, by the time the dog is about 12 months or more of age, the skeleton has largely ceased growing. (However, the Orthopaedic Foundation for Animals (OFA) scheme in the USA is after two years of age.)

Attempts have been made to make certifications internationally recognised, particularly in Europe. The disadvantage of all schemes is that, as young animals cannot be accurately screened, animals for breeding may have to be reared until they are adult before a final decision as to their breeding potential can be made.

Because there are variations in the expression of dysplasia and because some degree of HD is very common, the aim of all screening programmes has been to grade the amount of HD that is present. This relies on the principle of: the poorer the parent, the poorer the progeny; conversely, the better the parent, the better the progeny.

In some breeds, it is almost impossible to find a completely normal (perfect) animal so that, to some extent, animals with HD have to be bred. There is the added complication that, in dog breeding, selection of animals is based on a number of desired characteristics, and animals with good hips may, for example, have genetically poor eyes, or inherited problems with other joints, such as elbows or knees.

EXAMINATION PROCESS

The basic X-ray examination is similar for most schemes. For health and safety reasons, the animal must be suitably restrained, either under sedation or anaesthesia, so that the dog can be carefully positioned. X-rays are then made in one or more positions.

To prevent malpractice by dishonest breeders, some

form of identification is required to ensure that an X-ray belongs to a particular animal. Imprinting the film with the registration number of the dog and possibly a microchip or tattoo number is required, as well as the date of examination.

In the UK, the examination is controlled under the British Veterinary Association/Kennel Club scheme. For this scheme, a single view is made, with the dog lying on his back with the hind legs extended backwards and with the knee joints rotated inwards. This gives a good view of the femur head and neck, and allows any laxity to be assessed.

In some other countries, a second view, the 'frog leg' view, is also used, in which the hind legs are put in a flexed position. This view allows different regions of the femur head and neck to be visualised in a skyline projection, but laxity is poorly assessed.

EVALUATING X-RAYS

Radiographs are examined under all schemes to look for three basic types of change. Any changes seen are then measured in some way – either by giving a numerical score or by classifying the change according to agreed criteria. These examinations are generally made by individual vets who have some specific specialised radiological skill. Each film may be evaluated by one or more vets, working either together or independently.

1. Any signs of laxity, which is assessed by the amount of displacement of the femur head from the acetabulum. This can be done in a number of ways.

• Measurements of the highest and lowest points of the acetabulum allow one to estimate their depth (the Rhodes Jenny index)

• The most commonly used method is probably to

calculate the Norberg Olsson angle. The centre of each femur head is identified using a clear plastic overlay marked with rings, and the angle between these points and the outermost point on the acetabulum is measured with a protractor. A measurement of 105 degrees + is agreed to be ideal.

2. The overall conformation of the hip joint is assessed by evaluating the shapes of the various parts of the femur head and the acetabulum.

To some extent, this will be affected by the individual breed of the dog.

3. Any signs of degenerative joint disease (DJD) resulting from HD are estimated.

These are areas of the joint edge that have become worn away, or new bone that has been deposited around the edge of the acetabulum, on the femur head, or infilling the deeper parts of the acetabulum.

The various criteria are then assessed collectively to arrive at some method of grading. These grades vary from country to country. In the UK, the scheme results in each hip being awarded a numerical score, and the score from each joint is added to provide an overall score. An absolutely perfect dog would have a score of 0:0 = total 0. A most severely affected dog would have a score totalling 106.

In other countries, the final assessment is made on a more subjective basis with animals being allocated into about five groups. The boundaries between each group vary somewhat but are based on:

- Normal
- Borderline
- Mild

ASSESSING X-RAYS

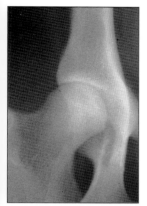

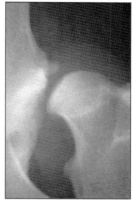

Normal left hip of a Rottweiler. The femur head is circular and well seated, with more than 50 per cent contained within the acetabulum. The joint edges are clean and clearly outlined.

Moderate to severe dysplasia. The joint of this 14-month-old Rottweiler is completely displaced from the acetabulum, which is infilled with new bone. New bone is also present at the edge of the joint and on the femur head and neck.

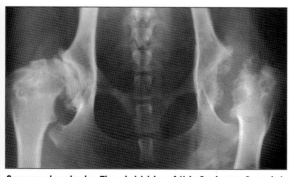

Severe dysplasia. The right hip of this Springer Spaniel has had a femoral head resection but the result was poor and the hip now needs replacing. The left hip has severe arthritic change with extensive remodelling of the femur head and neck, and a very narrowed joint space indicates erosion of the articular cartilage.

- Moderate
- Severe.

Because of the problem of trying to separate the effects of the genotype from the phenotype, which is what is seen on X-rays, there have been some new ideas to try to evaluate the primary defect – joint laxity.

The Penn Scheme, devised at the University of Pennsylvania, uses a method of stressing the hips to calculate the amount by which a joint can be displaced. Two X-ray views are made in different positions, and measurements of the position of the femur head is made. In this scheme, the evaluation is only based on the laxity of the joint.

Most other schemes evaluate laxity only on the appearance of the unstressed joint, but also include an assessment of the amount of secondary remodelling or arthritic change to reach the overall final conclusion. There is controversy here as to the importance of visible bony changes, as it appears that some dogs are genetically more likely to show bony changes in response to laxity while other animals do not.

SELECTION FOR BREEDING

Choosing the dog to breed and the animal not to use remains a very difficult problem. Some animals may have many excellent features, but perhaps have poor hips, while others may have wonderful hip joints but be poor in other respects (e.g. poor temperament, deafness, etc.). Thus one may often have to include animals that have some degree of HD in a breeding programme.

A second problem is that screening schemes pick out animals that are affected on the basis of their X-ray appearance, and this is not a perfect science. Generally, 'normal' animals have no signs of HD at all, i.e. they are 'perfect'. In practice, the number of perfect animals is very small and the number of perfect animals with no other problems is even smaller. Therefore, one frequently ends up using animals that have some HD.

Different countries give differing advice to breeders. Mostly, breeders are advised to use animals that fall into the 'normal' or 'borderline' categories. This can still be a problem in some dog breeds, because the number of animals in the breed that lie within those categories may be very small.

In the UK, the concept of the 'breed mean score' BMS is used. An average score is calculated from all the X-rays submitted in each breed and this score is published regularly by the British Veterinary Association (BVA). Copies of the most recent score sheet can be obtained from the BVA. General advice is to try to use animals that have a score that lies at or below the breed mean. In breeds with a low incidence of HD, the BMS will be low, but in breeds with a high incidence of HD, it will be higher. This will have the effect that animals with a greater degree of HD will be bred in breeds with a high BMS. The long-term effect of this is that the incidence of HD may only reduce slowly in these breeds.

VALUE OF SCHEMES

The success of any control scheme in reducing the degree and overall incidence of hip dysplasia will depend on breeders using their national scheme and prospective dog owners seeking puppies from screened stock with only a low-grade of dysplasia themselves.

Only very few countries or breeds insist on breeding stock being screened and many animals continue to be bred from unscreened parents throughout the world.

In many countries, control schemes are voluntary. The stimulus to increase screening will only come if purchasers more actively seek puppies from screened breeding stock and are prepared to pay breeders a premium for such puppies.

Because screening is not an exact science and the genotype and phenotype are not identical, some puppies will continue to have HD although they come from screened stock. However, in general, the chance of obtaining an affected puppy is reduced if screened stock is used. The accuracy of screening depends on the number of animals in a breed being checked.

It is of great advantage to screen animals that are probably not going to be used for breeding themselves. Comparison of as many related animals as possible enables the genotype of a dog to be more accurately assessed. In dog breeding, the male is more important than the female, as sires tend to mate with more than one bitch. Thus the effect of the male is greater. When sufficient puppies from one sire have been produced, it becomes possible to analyse the quality of the hips of the progeny and occasionally a sire possessing apparently good hips may, in fact, produce poor puppies with a high incidence of HD. Such a sire analysis will then enable the animal to be withdrawn from breeding. This analysis is only possible if enough puppies are assessed to be statistically significant.

When purchasing a puppy, research from the breed club and on the internet will usually be helpful. It remains important to see the parents if possible. Ask to see the certificates of screening for inherited diseases of both parents. If the ancestors of the parents have been screened too, then this information is also helpful to reduce the chance of a defective puppy.